Kamala Harris Kids

Blake LeVine+Ryan Arthur LeVine

Story Of Kamala Harris Kids

I began this book, after 5 years of raising a special needs child. It took me away from my comfort zone, and changed my idea of life. My son, Ryan Arthur LeVine was very different than my first child. He was often not looking into one's eyes and rarely speaking. We feared, autism or a severe mental illness.

I live with bipolar disorder and spent a few years in and out of psychiatric hospitals. My wife's uncle was at an Ivy League School studying to be a Doctor. He fell apart, and within a short time was diagnosed with schizophrenia. He died, last year while spending most of his adulthood in a permanent mental institution.

My dream, is to ask a higher power to save my son. How would this work? Is it possible to change a life, when you start at the earliest of ages? Did my books, videos, and presentations about bipolar teach youth, and also give me tools to overcome my son's differences? How would I look at being a dad, while dreaming daily of a successful adult life for my young child? I will admit, my childhood was incredibly weird. I came from a divorced family that had a large amount of abuse. I was kidnapped, for ten months at age 3 by my father. I eventually, had parents that made peace for the sake of their son. I won't say everything, but there was physical, psychological and pressure ramped up on everyone involved. The fighting, created a scared child that never could feel trust in life. I worked on it during years of therapy, only to learn the scarring in my earliest years became my truth.

I'd visit my dad, and spent up to seven hours a day, training to play high level baseball. I found, myself fascinated by meeting pro athletes starting at age 6. I developed, a passion for obtaining autographs and pictures with many of the legendary sports heroes. They include Mickey Mantle, Ted Williams, Joe DiMaggio, Michael Jordan, Larry Bird, Charles Barkley, Willie Mays, Bo Jackson, Deion Sanders, Joe Namath, and many others.

I transitioned, into meeting music, acting, politicians, and historical figures. I was fascinated, with their achievements. Why does, someone have a gift that is shareable with the whole world? What does it take to win an Academy Award, complete a stadium world tour, be elected President, or be remembered in the encyclopedia ? Does the gift develop through practice, patience or lifelong luck?

I ended up by age 15, being invited to personally meet President Clinton in the Oval Office. It was a top news story, that a young man with persistence would attract an invitation from The President himself. It wasn't a clear win, as some were angry I made profits from selling some of my autographs. They didn't agree that dedicating all your time to something, should earn the way a paperboy or other ambitious youngster learns about money.

The names in my photograph collection, are something I am proud of. I turned, 40 this year and realize a legacy was created. I view, the photographs and remember these moments in time. They include Mother Teresa and Princess Diana (on the same day), The Dalai Lama, Steven Spielberg, Tom Hanks, Ella Fitzgerald, B.B. King, Patrick Swayze, Audrey Hepburn, Lou Reed, Bob Dylan, Madonna, Michael Jackson, Harrison Ford, Will Smith, Spike Lee, Les Paul, Bill Hanna, Joe Barbera, Mikhail Gorbachev, Robin Williams, David Bowie, Notorious BIG, Jimmy Stewart, Gene Kelly, Julia Roberts, Farrah Fawcett, Aretha Franklin, Whitney Houston, and over 4,000 others.

I bring this introduction to explain, my goal of writing Kamala's Kids with my son. He has defied the odds, in incredible ways. We started to place him with therapy and support at age 2. He began to speak and progress with the weekly support. I would, encourage him to go to 2 years of special needs schooling in Florida to help him begin to be a student. He now speaks with a vocabulary on grade level. This year, he was transitioned into a school for students with no classifications. He did, incredibly well and is finishing his school year next week.

I watched, many of his classmates that came to the United States from India. They, didn't always talk of the truth. It shares, that many had relatives with no clean water, barely enough money to eat, possibly being forced to beg without assistance and other real atrocities. The goal, is to offer their children a better life. It is one with college, careers, confidence and creation. The families and children hope, to live a life with financial and spiritual abundance. The fight for success depends on all of us, learning and growing together. We are the generation that may choose to

see Kamala Harris as our first Female President. We're possibly electing someone that fought for

justice while facing racism for an Indian and African American heritage. The dream doesn't die

unless someone kills it for you. I cannot say enough, how hard people try to hurt those fighting

for social justice.

I was told, Kamala Harris is releasing two books. I found, a website that shares events at

Barnes and Noble shops in Los Angeles. I was excited, on January 13, 2019 Kamala Harris

would be there. My son, and daughter took a long ride from San Diego with my wife Jen.

We camped out front seeing what it may look and feel like to be homeless. The day began,

by standing on the street covered in blankets, waiting with others, and hoping to be early enough

to go inside. Within, a few hours we were given wristbands and gained access to the signing.

How would she be? Would my son, be calm enough to listen to her sharing her book? Did
Ryan's

first autograph change our destiny and maybe the world's? Would he have been chosen, to share

his book despite struggling to write? Would my son and I work together in our own way, to say

Kamala's Kids are here to stay? Do we need a group of kids that are willing to hold hands with

any type of person? Does racism, hatred, fear, and depression need to be lifted from all of our

lives?

The idea presented, is to share the greatness of those I personally met. The goal, is to write a series that is released in different editions. We have decided each one, will have 3 figures in each title.

I spoke to my son today about our work. He had just finished school, when we went to have a pizza. He wouldn't put on his shoes and walked into the restaurant in his green socks. The woman working there, seemed tired and warm. The air wasn't great on a hot day in California. My son, went up to her and said "How do you make the pizza"? She smiled as this working mom, finished preparing the dough.

They ended up spending 20 minutes talking, laughing and having fun. Her kindness, glistened as she told us about her own child being speech delayed. We connected, through the gregarious nature of a young man.

My son and I began to speak about how to write together. I asked him about kindness for the chapter on Kamala Harris. He said "I like kindness". I realized, his ideas are sometimes simple but truthful. The books would be both easy to understand and documentary pictures. We figure, illustrations of actual photographs are beautiful and unique.

It is our greatest gift, to learn and create openness. My son, has showed me that a slower life may be progress. I see him, going at his own pace and deserving energy for his ideas. I now know, that God makes everyone in their own way. I trust, with a prayer and a dream there are no failures. The success, is admitting the journey is always just one small step at a time.

I don't know why but a dark cloud, has taken away many that struggle with mental illness and special needs. I propose, a way to inspire and create change. We elect leaders that love helping all of us; We're proud to be different and celebrate success. Our economy booms, when we see everyone actually achieving their dreams. We bring back wealth to the middle class, and make us healthier, happier and our own hero. Kamala Harris is willing to try, and you better believe so am I! Even with a spelling error, my son has taught me to never quit! We shall win with bravery, brilliance and understanding ourselves.

CHAPTERS

Kamala Harris

Elton John

Patrick Swayze

Kamala Harris

Kamala Harris taught us about kindness. She shows that inside all of our brains, is a gift of being nice to others. We met her, while she read her book to children. It was at the Barnes and Noble in Los Angeles, California. There was one girl who could not walk, and was sitting in a wheelchair. Kamala, stood up to speak to her and sign her autograph. It showed, Kindness with a capital K.

We know, she may be the first Female President. Ryan thought, his mom is the President of our house. She works, and is always in charge. I feel being kind is a gift that keeps on giving. I hope, Kamala Harris is President and brings peace and prosperity to all people.

Presidential Candidate Kamala, has family from Jamaica. When Ryan comes home from school, I give him a fist bump and we say "Respect". I learned, it when I went to Ochos Rios and Negril, Jamaica. Ryan taught the kids in his class, kindness and respect are cool for Kamala and us.

BARNES & NOBLE
Events
GWYNETH PALTROW
BARNES & NOBLE
Events
KAMALA HARRIS
BARNES & NOBLE
Events
KAMALA HARRIS

BARNES&NOBLE
BOOKSELLERS

BARNES&NOBLE
BOOKSELLERS

BARNES&NOBLE
BOOKSELLERS
Events
KAMA
SUPERHEROES Are Everywhere
KAMALA HARRIS

BARNES&NOBLE
BOOKSELLERS

Elton John

I sing songs with my son all the time. The connection, we have to music grows with each year.

Our day was filled with happiness, singing The Itsy Bitsy Spider song together on an overcast

day this week. The movie Rocketman, was just released here in the United States. I told my son,

that Elton John is a living legend. His soulful songs, depict a generation that found inspiration

with his classic hits.

When I was a little older than my son, I began to meet music stars. I knew, Elton John was one
of

the most famous alive. I found out, from a famous collector that he would be at his hotel in New

York City. We had some vintage albums that were large and colorful. They were heavy but fun
to

view.

When Elton John, was coming into the hotel he seemed shy and reserved. I asked for his

autograph, and he was incredibly kind to sign. The aura of him was one of the greatest lessons I

learned. It is the word, self esteem. He chose, to be himself and not always have to be perfectly

boisterous I just asked my son if he understands about self esteem. Ryan shared, that he likes

himself. I admitted, that is the exact idea of the term. We may be different, loud (as Ryan often

is), cautious, flamboyant, or frigid and it is at times what we are willing to share. I see life, with a

version of optimism thanks to Sir Elton John.

He carefully demonstrated that a musical superstar may come in all shapes and forms. I

witnessed, Robert Plant with his wild curly hair, Keith Richards tattooed and smoking, Little

Richard howling

out of a limousine window all with their rock god personas. Elton showed my boy Ryan and I to

give a little respect as Aretha Franklin would admire. The self esteem, you developed is based on

loving and accepting yourself all throughout the journey.

Patrick Swayze

My wife and Ryan's grandmother passed away several years ago. Her greatest pleasure,

was watching Dirty Dancing with her daughter Jen (my wife). They said, the movie connected

with them them on an emotional level that made Patrick Swayze her hero.

I told her, about my special experiences meeting Patrick Swayze and his wife Lisa. The first

time, occurred on a school vacation break. I went, to Hollywood, California looking to obtain

autographs. I went to the set on Beverly Hills, 90210, visited Spago's meeting stars and read that

Patrick Swayze was appearing on The Tonight Show.

We went to the Burbank studios and there was no access. I was sad, but decided to wait where

the gate was. I was thrilled and shocked, when a town car came out with Patrick Swayze. He

rolled down the window, and told the driver to pull over. His energy, was loving and beautiful.

Patrick gladly signed a few autographs and posed for pictures.

I would again see him, in one of the funniest situations. I heard, they were filming a movie called

Thanks For Everything, Too Wong Foo. It had several major stars, but I learned they would all

be dressed as women. I don't hate crossdressers at all, but didn't know what to expect. They

were filming at a nightclub in Manhattan. I went to the location hoping for some pictures and

autographs.

While I was waiting, I heard the cast was filming inside. I couldn't go in, but hoped he may sign on the way out. I watched as a voluptuous looking woman walked out with a few guards. It was Patrick Swayze in drag! He had heels, tons of eye makeup, and a dress. Who would of expected this!

I calmly, walked up to him and asked for his autograph. He seemed a little embarrassed and said "Kid can I get dressed and then come out and sign"? I said, "Sure, sir". He had me wait by his trailer for about 10 minutes. He exited, looking like the man my mother in law loved. This time, he had on no shirt, was buff and flashing his million dollar smile. He posed for photographs, signed autographs and was awesome! There ended up being a large crowd when women noticed a hunky Patrick, shirtless and standing on a Manhattan street.

My son and I talked about the virtue of creativity. Ryan, wasn't in a great mood and sad dance is "bad". I then, realized he wanted to spend time with his mom who had a very long day at work. I thought to myself about Patrick's creative gifts. I had read, he once gained a part he wasn't capable of. He told a fib, but worked super hard when he was finally granted the role. It led, to him eventually being a star. I then, understood about his career highs and lows.

The icon, wasn't always given A list pictures even though Dirty Dancing will be around forever. It takes, creativity to play a woman and be fun during the adventure of filming. I met, him a few other times when his wife Lisa Niemi was starring in a Broadway show. He would hang out with her after each performance. Patrick was never too special to not support her goals as well.

I told Ryan, I feel loving someone with all your heart is creative. It takes, courage and confidence

to keep going and growing in all parts of life. I believe, Patrick Swayze lived and died with self

respect and grace. The charm he always emanated, lit up in Dirty Dancing. I see, Lisa struggling

at losing her love and it harming her family. He dedicated his life, to creating pictures that

moved. The light on screen, will beam bright forever.